I SPY
EASTER
WITH MY LITTLE EYE

D1498251

AGES 2-5

Little Cat Press

How to play

- Find an object in the picture that start with the given letter.
- Flip the page to see if you're a winner with the answer key.
- Color the objects once found.

Have a blast!

Little Cat Press

I Spy with my little eye
something beginning with...

Basket

I Spy with my little eye
something beginning with...

Chick

I Spy with my little eye
something beginning with...

I Spy with my little eye something beginning with...

Egg

I Spy with my little eye something beginning with...

I Spy with my little eye
something beginning with...

Gift

I Spy with my little eye
something beginning with...

Hat

I Spy with my little eye something beginning with...

I Spy with my little eye
something beginning with...

Kite

I Spy with my little eye
something beginning with...

Leaf

I Spy with my little eye
something beginning with...

Mouse

I Spy with my little eye something beginning with...

Nut

I Spy with my little eye something beginning with...

Owl

Pen

I Spy with my little eye something beginning with...

Quill

I Spy with my little eye
something beginning with...

I Spy with my little eye
something beginning with...

I Spy with my little eye
something beginning with...

Vase

I Spy with my little eye
something beginning with...

I Spy with my little eye
something beginning with...

Xylophone

I Spy with my little eye
something beginning with...

Yoga

I Spy with my little eye something beginning with...

Made in United States
North Haven, CT
03 April 2023

34984158R00059